Dear women,

Please take good care of yourself. Put your needs before the needs of your significant others.

Love you above everything else. Men are built differently so they love us far different than we love them.

DIVORCE CHRONICLES

Monica S. Martinez

Tantalizing Productions, Inc.

Copyright © 2018 by Monica S. Martinez

All rights reserved. No part of this book may be reproduced in any form or by any means without the prior written consent of the Publisher.

If you purchase this book without a cover you should be aware that this book has both been stolen and reported as "unsold and destroyed" to the publisher. In such case neither the author nor the publisher has received payment for this "stripped book".

This story is a work of fiction. Names characters, places and incidents as well as any resemblance to actual persons, living or dead is coincidental.

CONTENT WARNING

This book contains strong language of sexual content and violence. It is intended for mature audiences only.

ISBN-13: 978-0-9841573-6-5
Cover Design: Jeannette Mobley
Editors: Marty Gonzales

Acknowledgements

I want to take a moment and thank God for the journey he has set me on. Without his mercy I wouldn't be able to do this thing I love. Writing for me has always been my saving grace. To my children, you are the reason I strive to be better every day. For my rock, my best friend – my husband, I thank you for standing by me with me through it all. I love you.

To my sisters, I thank each and every one of you for supporting my journey in this writing field. I thank you all for giving me the motivation to keep writing. You ladies say you're my number one fans – well it's the other way around, I'm your number one fan, each and everyone one of you. I'm truly blessed to have you all by my side. To my mother whom I've witnessed experience her own divorce pain, I say to you thank you for being so vulnerable showing us it's okay. I love you.

Well, Jeannette Mobley you know this book couldn't be a book without your loving touch. You never let me down and that I'm forever grateful for.

To all my supporters I thank you and know that I do this for you!

Dedication

This book is dedicated to all the women who have experienced the pain of Divorce or for those who are on the verge of Divorce. This book will take you through the emotions of love, pain, anger, finding self- love and will remind you of what your happiness will look like. Never lose yourself!

Introduction

We take vows till death do us part and for better or worse. Is a marriage able to withstand temptation? What will you do when it comes knocking? Will you fight to the bitter end? Or will walk and throw away everything you shared?

DIVORCE CHRONICLES

I looked at him with love as he looked past me
unable to bring that loving look back in his eyes
Struggling to keep this lie together
Hoping we could be happy once again
The pain is filling up inside my heart
The inner voice yelling we must part
Not wanting to let him go
Afraid of being alone
Yet I'm lonely when he's there
Walking pass a mirror in fear
Facing truths I didn't dare
This broken heart can't mend So I bend and bend
Hoping he wakes up
But I'm broken
He doesn't even take notice
Silently I stay Praying for a miracle
But I keep going in circles
Round and round
Scared to step out of the box
Emotionally dependent
Wanting to scream I love you
So he could hear it clearly
Because it feels like it's going on deaf ears
Whispering in the middle of the night
We could win this fight
I'm not built for this battle
The mirror is shattering
Picking up these pieces

Knowing it will never be the same
It's a shame if all these years
go down the drain
I'm straining to keep it together As tears stain my face
This is the story of one who loves the other more
Because love is never equal
Feeling doubtful as the sun rises
And I rise To face the man I don't want to replace

*The start of the hurt can be devastating.
Especially when it catches you off guard.*

Never remind him how to treat you.
He knew how when he was pursuing you.

_____
_____
_____
_____
_____
_____
_____
_____
_____
_____
_____

Monica S. Martinez

*I walked past the closet
that was filled with his skeletons
without realizing it.*

They say all great things
must come to an end!
The end has approached!

*Love was noticeable on both of us-
Temptation came at a heavy price!*

Divorce Chronicles

*I used to text him throughout the day
to remind him I loved him.*

_____
_____
_____
_____
_____
_____
_____
_____
_____
_____

Monica S. Martinez

*Marriage was a piece of paper to him.
For me it was the magic of our love
for eternity!*

Divorce Chronicles

Love left his lips loosely!

*His love lifted me.
I thought I was in heaven
– but it was all an illusion!*

Divorce Chronicles

*I felt a shift
in the relationship!*

_____
_____
_____
_____
_____
_____
_____
_____
_____
_____
_____

His infidelity poured out of my body.

It was the way he held me that had me fooled!

Monica S. Martinez

*I looked at him with love beaming
– while he looked past me!*

Divorce Chronicles

*I was starved for his attention,
so I took it in spurts*

_____
_____
_____
_____
_____
_____
_____
_____
_____
_____

Monica S. Martinez

He ignored my love!

*I wore a ring of an eternity
filled with deception!*

*He rocked a wedding ring
even though it meant nothing to him.
You see, vows were meant to be broken!*

Laying next to him
— I felt as if we were miles apart!

Monica S. Martinez

*His "I love you's" were consistent
but so were his lies!*

*His phone stayed on silent
when he was home.
I always wanted to know why?*

Monica S. Martinez

When I asked him a question
– deception was at the tip of his tongue!

Divorce Chronicles

We vowed till death do us part.
The only thing dying was my heart!

*The lies have begun and the pain starts.
He's hurting you more and more!
You want to scream so he can hear you.
But he has you muted
with his tunnel vision!*

Divorce Chronicles

*Living a double life made him
a master of fabrication*

Monica S. Martinez

The truth couldn't come from him because lying was a habit!

*He held me tight at night
just to sleep better.
I guess it was from all the lies
he was telling!
Maybe I'd believe that he loved me!*

*He spoke sweetly to everyone else
– guess he forgot his manners
for his own home!*

Divorce Chronicles

*He never meant to hurt me.
Yet the tears steadily rolled
down my face daily!*

He said it was in your mind.
That you were just making it up.
In reality, it was your gut instinct speaking
directly to you when he was cheating!
Never ignore your gut.

Dirty laundry aired in the mist of perceived happiness!

DIVORCE CHRONICLES

Two ships passing
Wondering when did it become this way
Kisses no longer are given at the sight of one another
More like roommates than lovers
Back pressed up against spine
Sleeping without touching
Restless nights staring into the skylight
Reminiscing of a love that we once shared
When did it become that we no longer care?
This relationship is on shaky ground
Not a peep not even a sound
Temptation becoming our playground
Our backyard filled with lust
Trusting becomes more of an issue
Suspicious of every move
Clueless on how to bring it back together
Never expecting the storm that's brewing
Separation looming
Is the relationship doomed?
No room for repair
But who dare be the one to make mention?
In need of his attention
Desperate pleas for his affection
Wearing his favorite piece to sleep
Him never taking notice
This is the final notice, our relationship
is hanging on the edge
Realizing I'm falling off the cliff
Without him offering his hand
The truth hurts

He no longer feels No longer see's me No longer loves
Yearning for someone else; attention diverted
The grass appears greener on the other side
Contemplating whether or not he should take the ride
Not realizing he will lose the ultimate prize
My eyes searching for vindication
His eyes closed refusing to give resolution
Our institution of marriage
No longer filled with laughter
No longer filled with communication No relations
History is closing in on our chapters
Ending the story of what once was love
Happily ever after null and void
Trying to avoid the inevitable
The cards are on the table, no shuffle required
Afraid to turn one over because the joker may appear
The end is near
Not sparing one's feelings
Forcing it to be finally dealt with
Infidelity looms
Dark gray skies as we look up praying for relief
Ready to unleash pain which will be unbearable
Becoming the death of relationship salvation
Is there light at the end of the tunnel?
One wonders
When will the pain subside?
Heart wilting like a flower
that no longer wishes to bloom

Monica S. Martinez

He said he wouldn't do
anything to jeopardize me!
Yet he compromised our marriage!

Divorce Chronicles

He said he wasn't obligated to wear his wedding ring.

_____
_____
_____
_____
_____
_____
_____
_____
_____
_____
_____
_____

He took our love out of content!

I didn't know how to be selfish like him!

Feeling the depth of his lies!

Divorce Chronicles

*I loved before. I've experienced pain
– but not like this!*

The pain was a lonely path to walk.
I was on this journey by myself.
I wanted to reach for him
but knew I'd drown.

He tried to test the boundaries of our marriage with his disrespect!

Monica S. Martinez

He was giving his attention to another while I was seeking his attention!

Betrayal isn't for the weak!

His only regret is that he got caught!

His love wasn't unconditional he was conditioned to cheat!

*He was busy
entertaining someone else.*

Divorce Chronicles

His love for me was temporary!
Marriage wasn't forever!

_____
_____
_____
_____
_____
_____
_____
_____
_____
_____
_____
_____

*The excuses now come into play.
What will you do with the truth
that you know in your heart of hearts?*

*He said he loved me but
just wasn't in love with me anymore!
I stood still as his tongue cut me in half.
The tears came rushing down my face
as my dignity was taken from me!*

My heart is broken and I'm not sure if I can mend the pieces back together!

*I prayed on empty prayers
to my God!
My husband didn't bother
praying for us!*

Monica S. Martinez

I looked in the mirror and realized I was lost!

Divorce Chronicles

If love is blind
— why did I see his true colors?

Monica S. Martinez

Rejection is a hard pill to swallow!

_____
_____
_____
_____
_____
_____
_____
_____
_____
_____
_____

Relationships take two participants who are willing to do the work. He didn't believe in putting in the effort.

_____
_____
_____
_____
_____
_____
_____
_____
_____
_____

Monica S. Martinez

His eyes told me a different story!

Finding out love was one-sided is hard!

Forever was never intended as far as he was concerned!
Those were just words in our vows!

*He wanted to be married
only with single capabilities!*

Monica S. Martinez

Looking in the mirror – I asked myself when did I become the needy one?

Divorce Chronicles

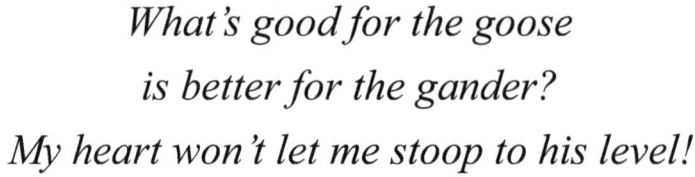

*What's good for the goose
is better for the gander?
My heart won't let me stoop to his level!*

_____
_____
_____
_____
_____
_____
_____
_____
_____
_____
_____

Monica S. Martinez

I was breaking so I needed him to hold me.
Even though I knew it was a lie!

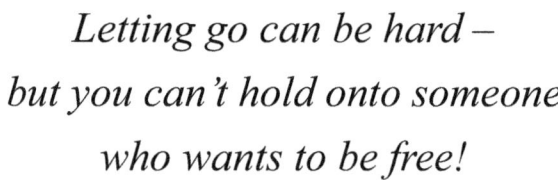

*Letting go can be hard –
but you can't hold onto someone
who wants to be free!*

*She has fully entered the picture.
You want to fight for him because he is your
husband. But will he fight for you?*

Divorce Chronicles

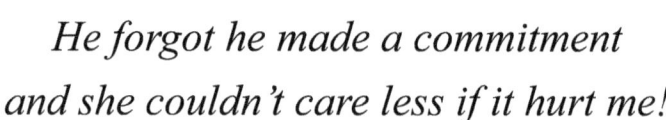

*He forgot he made a commitment
and she couldn't care less if it hurt me!*

_____
_____
_____
_____
_____
_____
_____
_____
_____
_____

Monica S. Martinez

Her scent lingered.

Divorce Chronicles

I didn't want to let him go!

Monica S. Martinez

I dreamed of a life with him
– but he wanted the best of both worlds!

Divorce Chronicles

The thought of him calling her beautiful called for my insecurities!

_____
_____
_____
_____
_____
_____
_____
_____
_____
_____

Imagining him touching her
the way he touched me
made me fall to my knees.
I begged God to take the pain away!

Divorce Chronicles

*I found myself calling her only to hang up!
I just wanted to hear
what she sounded like!*

Monica S. Martinez

Shattered dreams of my happiness!

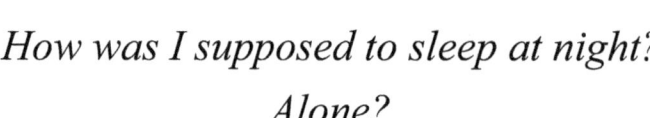

How was I supposed to sleep at night?
Alone?

_____
_____
_____
_____
_____
_____
_____
_____
_____
_____
_____

Monica S. Martinez

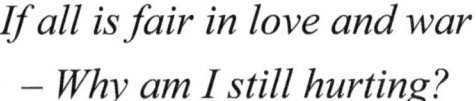

*If all is fair in love and war
— Why am I still hurting?*

Divorce Chronicles

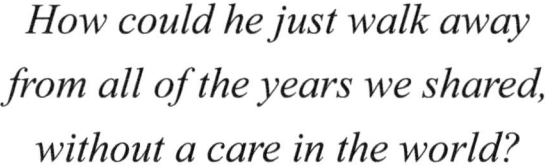

*How could he just walk away
from all of the years we shared,
without a care in the world?*

Monica S. Martinez

I loved him more than he loved me!

Divorce Chronicles

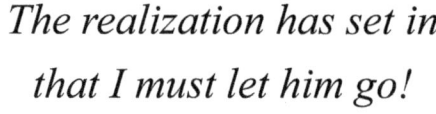

The realization has set in that I must let him go!

_____
_____
_____
_____
_____
_____
_____
_____
_____
_____

*When he realizes the grass isn't greener
on the other side.
Will I be long gone and healed?
I need answers, now!*

Divorce Chronicles

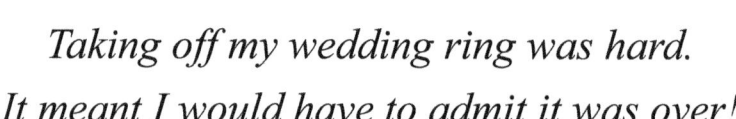

*Taking off my wedding ring was hard.
It meant I would have to admit it was over!*

_____
_____
_____
_____
_____
_____
_____
_____
_____
_____

Monica S. Martinez

*He remembered he loved me,
when he realized I was getting used
to the fact he didn't want me!*

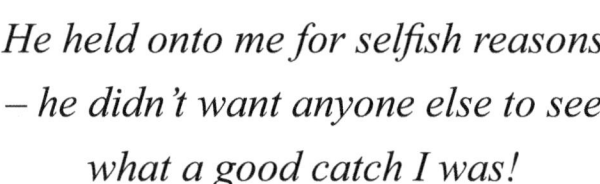

*He held onto me for selfish reasons
– he didn't want anyone else to see
what a good catch I was!*

_____
_____
_____
_____
_____
_____
_____
_____
_____
_____

Are mistakes really just mistakes?
What will you do when he tells you
he made just that?

Divorce Chronicles

I still love him!

Monica S. Martinez

He wanted another chance.
He promised he would make it work!

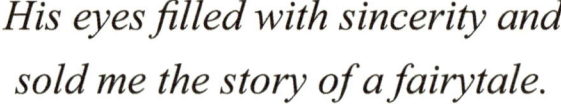

His eyes filled with sincerity and sold me the story of a fairytale.

*Second chances leave room
for resentment!*

Divorce Chronicles

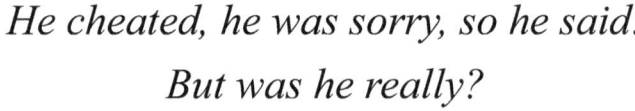

He cheated, he was sorry, so he said!
But was he really?

_____
_____
_____
_____
_____
_____
_____
_____
_____
_____

Monica S. Martinez

I had high hopes that we could fix it!

*I had to give it one last try.
My heart said I shouldn't
but I needed to for my own sanity.*

Monica S. Martinez

When he made love to me I couldn't bear to look him in the eyes. Even after I told him I forgave him and we would work on our marriage. All I saw was him making love to someone other than me

I imagined what she looked like!

Our love was toxic and I was infected with insecurities!

My heart had left him already and I continued to strain with the lie.

_____
_____
_____
_____
_____
_____
_____
_____
_____
_____
_____

He gave me what he could
– only I needed much more
since he destroyed our trust!

I eventually realized I was the fool!

*The worst thing you can do is
to fool yourself into thinking it can work!*

His love is what I thought I needed!

*The moment it hits you
- that you deserve way better
than what he's giving!
You've just had your epiphany!*

*The shift of power comes.
With this power comes
great responsibility to self!*

_____
_____
_____
_____
_____
_____
_____
_____
_____
_____

Walking Away!

Divorce Chronicles

The rebirth of finding me within myself was liberating. I realized how to love myself.

*Wanting & needing
are two different things!
I never needed him, I wanted him.*

*I never wanted him to complete me.
I just wanted him to love me!*

_____
_____
_____
_____
_____
_____
_____
_____
_____
_____

Monica S. Martinez

History is comforting!
But sometimes you need to re-write it!

I thought I needed his validation!

Monica S. Martinez

*His selfish ways should
have been a red flag!*

Divorce Chronicles

*I loved my self much more
than he ever knew!
I just had to remind myself of my worth!*

_____
_____
_____
_____
_____
_____
_____
_____
_____
_____

The truth hurts, but I'll take it over a lie!
The lying nearly killed me!

*Heartbreaks eventually heal.
Your shattered heart will mend
and you will love again!*

Monica S. Martinez

He didn't count his blessings when he had me!

*I knew my worth,
now he's suffering!*

*Don't chase a dream of fairy tales.
Love takes effort to build
a solid foundation!*

*I know our story had to end.
There's something better in the making!*

Pieces of me will remain with him!

Memories will take you through your past.
Remember your journey hasn't ended.

_____
_____
_____
_____
_____
_____
_____
_____
_____
_____
_____

Marriage is for lovers who put in the work! You must fulfill your obligations!

*Love can break your heart
but time will heal it.
Always be a lover of love and
never allow the pain to consume you!*

The pain is temporary!

*He will never change for you
in your current relationship.
He must lose you in order to change.
Unfortunately it makes him a better man for the
next relationship that comes along.
We set the tone for our relationship
if we keep accepting what they give,
and continue to forgive their actions
then we have to understand
it will continue to be the same.
When you value and love yourself you know
exactly what needs to be done!*

DIVORCE CHRONICLES

Looking into his eyes I see sadness
As I no longer believe his lies
Of the three words I longed to be true
When did I love you become a fad?

A saying with no depth
When did I lose myself within him?
All the excuses

Clueless of his deception that was staring me
right in the face
It's time for me to face my reality
Love is no longer patiently waiting
He's conflicted in his emotions
Wanting to leave me in limbo
Refusing to allow me to move on
I'm in search of closure

With my eyes closed
Blinded by what this heart feels
My inner-voice screaming for me to
WAKE UP
This is real...Not a nightmare

Our time has come to an end
No more pretend
This isn't a fairy tale Of which is told
"Happily Ever After" Can't be sold
Emotions will unfold

Tears flowing
Anger is roaring
Bringing out the worst in me
Smiles are no longer sparkling
He's taken my joy
Toying with my heart At my expense
Situation becoming more intense
No longer making sense

Fist flying
Crying tears of hurt
He's trying to divert my attention
By mentioning we could work it out
Maybe to buy more time

In search of his alibis
Realizing he's not dealing with an amateur
You see I've been on this road before
A life filled with lies
I'm in search of our final goodbye
There no sign of relief

Heart-shattering with disbelief
Didn't see this coming,
This storm High winds
Twister of hatred brewing oceans with waves of pain
I'm begging for the sun to shine
And my heart to be mine once again
The warrior in me must rise
And love me through my eyes

www.ingramcontent.com/pod-product-compliance
Lightning Source LLC
Chambersburg PA
CBHW051653040426
42446CB00009B/1124